*For Jelena, my grapefruit, Mom, Dad,
and all bunnies in the world*—Anton

Mina, Kian, and Milo—Anne

Explore the Ocean

Adventures Under the Sea with Emma and Louis

Text by Anne Ameri-Siemens
Illustrated by Anton Hallmann
Translated by Ryan Eyers

LITTLE
GESTALTEN

4

Off to the Oceans!

Humans have been fascinated by the world's oceans for thousands of years, and for just as long they've been traveling the seas and investigating the animals and plants that live underwater. It's no wonder, then, that Emma and Louis want to journey beneath the waves and explore, too! There are countless incredible creatures to see, both near the water's surface and down in the oceans' murky depths. On their journey, Emma and Louis will meet brave researchers—and even people who live on the ocean. What's more, they will learn about old legends of the seas, mysterious aquatic creatures, and the incredible landscapes that exist underwater.

One thing that particularly impressed them was this: life on Earth began billions of years ago in the ocean—which at the time was still one giant body of water. Like all life on Earth, we humans can trace our origins back to the first life-form that sprang into being then.

Did you know the Earth is also the only planet in the solar system with fluid water on its surface? If you look at it from space, the oceans appear blue. That's why Earth is sometimes called the "blue planet." Oceans are not only important because they contain so much beauty and so many things that inspire wonder, or because they're a fun place to swim, dive, surf, and discover, but because they also play an important role in regulating the Earth's climate.

Enough talk: come join us on our journey of discovery!

What Is an Ocean?

Seas and oceans contain salt water. Almost 97 percent of all water on Earth is salt water! The remaining fresh water can be found in lakes, rivers, groundwater, glaciers, and the polar ice caps.

The word *ocean* comes from the Greek. It was used in ancient times, back when people believed in Oceanus, a god who took the form of a river that flowed around the entire world.

The term "ocean" is used to label the enormous bodies of water that separate the Earth's continents.

Fresh water also contains salt, but only in very small amounts (less than 0.1 percent per liter).

LAKE SUPERIOR

LAKE BAIKAL

Lake Baikal in Russia is the world's deepest lake, with a maximum depth of almost 5,400 feet (1,642 meters). The largest freshwater lake on Earth is Lake Superior in North America, with a surface area of 31,700 square miles (82,103 square kilometers).

Salt water is no help when you're thirsty! Due to its high salt content (around 3.5 percent) it can even be dangerous to drink. This is because the more salt water you drink, the more your body loses water. Salt water is no problem for fish and other sea creatures, however, as they have adapted to their environment.

The ocean is filled with many millions of creatures that possess a very wide range of abilities. Many of these creatures are also essential for human life.

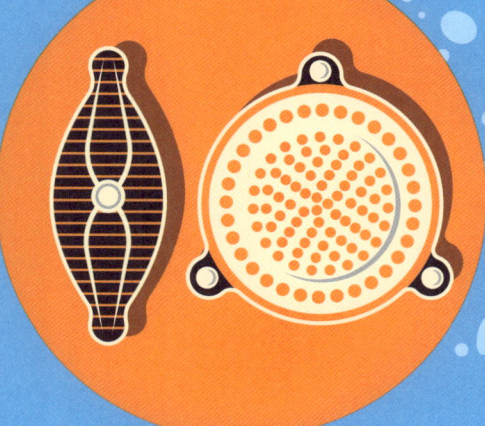

Silica algae (Diatoms)

These tiny life-forms are present in **plankton** and serve as food for many animals, such as whale sharks. Silica algae are smaller than the diameter of a human hair. Their cell walls consist of silicic acid, which is what gives them their name.

Boxer shrimp (Stenopodidea)

These small shrimps eat parasites and dead skin particles, which they seek out on the skin of **fish,** giving their temporary hosts a good clean in the process. This kind of relationship between animals is called cleaning symbiosis.

Whale (Cetacea)

Not only are **whales** impressively large, they are also important for ocean life as a whole. By diving down deep to feed and then returning to the surface for air, they help mix together the different layers of water that are rich and weak in **nutrients.** This is good for the life-forms that live in the oceans' depths. Whale excrement also serves as a fertilizer for phytoplankton (such as silica algae).

Giant oceanic manta ray (Mobula birostris)

This is the largest ray in the world and it is found in all tropical oceans. Giant oceanic manta ray feeds on plankton, sea urchins, small fish and starfish.

The Atlantic herring is one of the most commonly occurring fish species in the ocean. Herrings live in giant shoals. They are an important food source for many other species, such as whales, dolphins, sharks, and seabirds.

Prehistoric Oceans

Less than a third of our planet is covered by dry land, which is divided into a number of distinct segments: the seven continents. Many millions of years ago, there was only one continent, surrounded by one gigantic ocean.

Imagine for a moment: 205 million years ago, the region where the Alps now stand was at the bottom of a sea! Here, fossils of ichthyosaurs, which once lived in the ocean, have been found 9,100 feet (2,800 meters) above sea level.

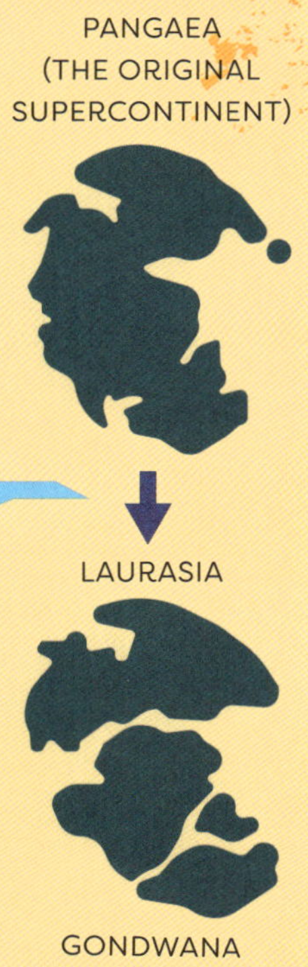

PANGAEA
(THE ORIGINAL
SUPERCONTINENT)

LAURASIA

GONDWANA

NORTH
AMERICA

EURASIA

INDIA

SOUTH
AMERICA

AFRICA

AUSTRALIA

ANTARCTICA

NORTH
AMERICA

EURASIA

INDIA

SOUTH
AMERICA

AFRICA

AUSTRALIA

ANTARCTICA

Formation of the continents

Around 250 million years ago, instead of seven separate continents, there was only one giant landmass: Pangaea. It was surrounded by a single ocean that spanned the globe: Panthalassa. Around 200 million years ago, Pangaea split into the continents Laurasia and Gondwana.

Laurasia later divided into the two continents of Eurasia and North America, while Gondwana fragmented into South America, Africa, Australia, and Antarctica, as well as the Indian subcontinent.

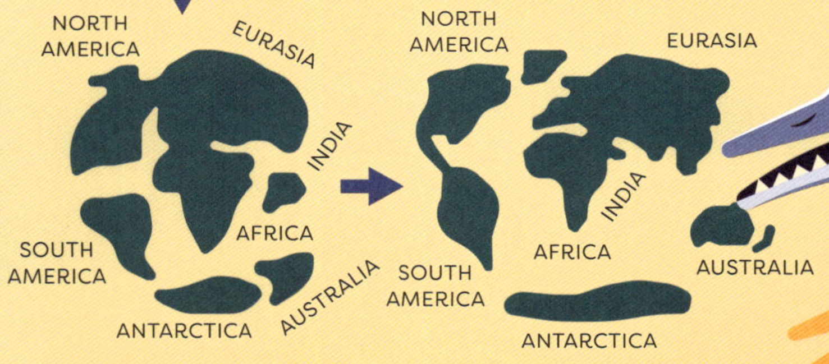

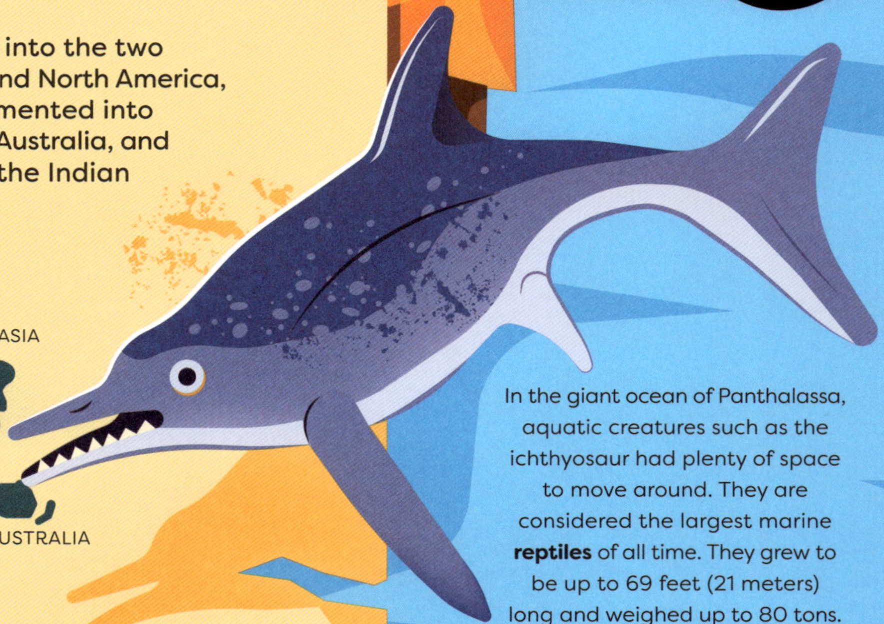

In the giant ocean of Panthalassa, aquatic creatures such as the ichthyosaur had plenty of space to move around. They are considered the largest marine **reptiles** of all time. They grew to be up to 69 feet (21 meters) long and weighed up to 80 tons.

Tectonic plates

The Earth's surface can be thought of as a giant jigsaw puzzle. The individual pieces are called tectonic plates, which together make up the entire surface of the Earth, divided into dry land and ocean floor. The tectonic plates move over the top of each other or away from each other (about as quickly as a fingernail grows). Sometimes they also collide with each other. This can result in the formation of mountains and volcanoes—as well as earthquakes.

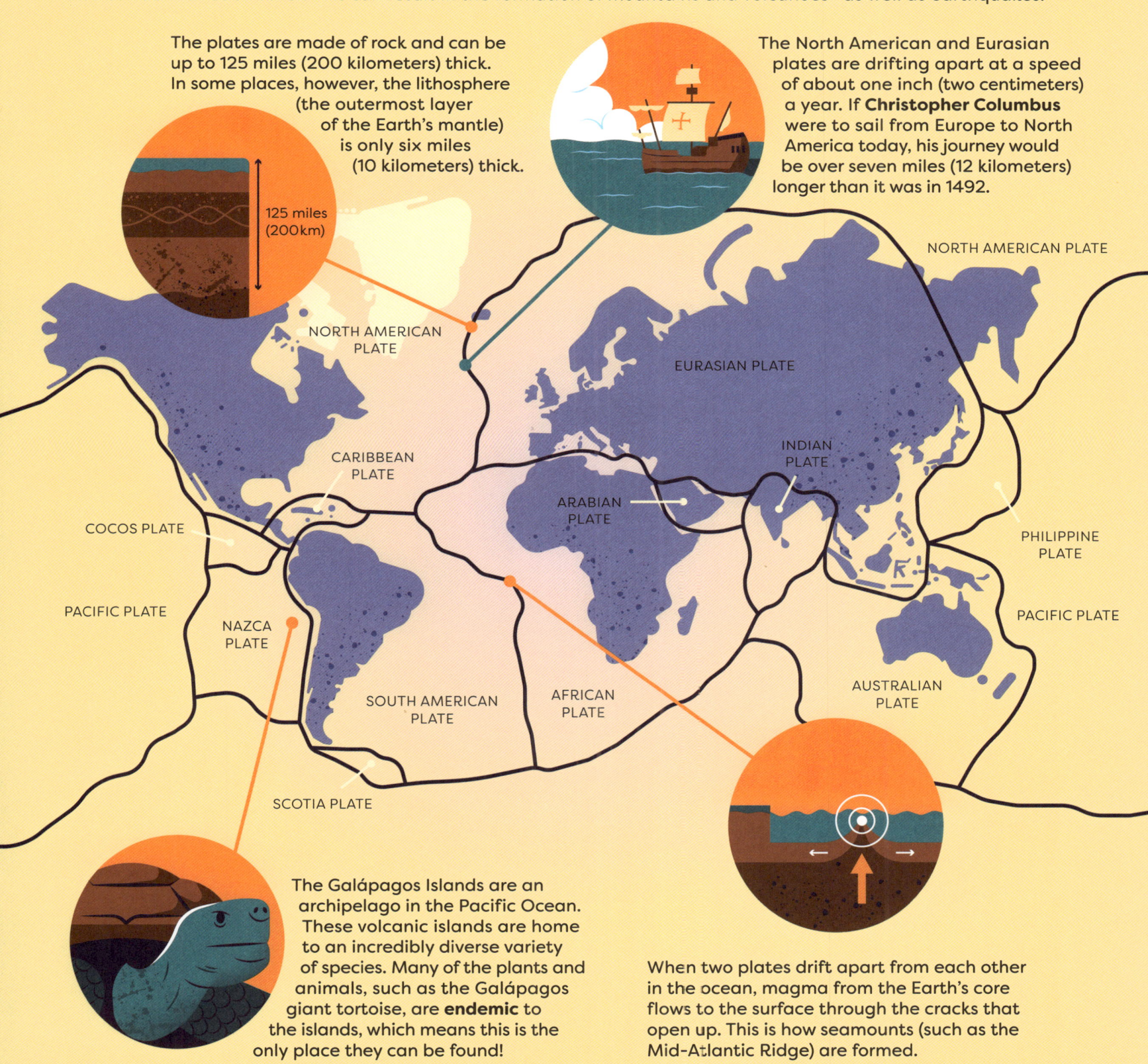

The plates are made of rock and can be up to 125 miles (200 kilometers) thick. In some places, however, the lithosphere (the outermost layer of the Earth's mantle) is only six miles (10 kilometers) thick.

125 miles (200km)

The North American and Eurasian plates are drifting apart at a speed of about one inch (two centimeters) a year. If **Christopher Columbus** were to sail from Europe to North America today, his journey would be over seven miles (12 kilometers) longer than it was in 1492.

NORTH AMERICAN PLATE

NORTH AMERICAN PLATE

EURASIAN PLATE

INDIAN PLATE

CARIBBEAN PLATE

ARABIAN PLATE

COCOS PLATE

PHILIPPINE PLATE

PACIFIC PLATE

PACIFIC PLATE

NAZCA PLATE

AUSTRALIAN PLATE

SOUTH AMERICAN PLATE

AFRICAN PLATE

SCOTIA PLATE

The Galápagos Islands are an archipelago in the Pacific Ocean. These volcanic islands are home to an incredibly diverse variety of species. Many of the plants and animals, such as the Galápagos giant tortoise, are **endemic** to the islands, which means this is the only place they can be found!

When two plates drift apart from each other in the ocean, magma from the Earth's core flows to the surface through the cracks that open up. This is how seamounts (such as the Mid-Atlantic Ridge) are formed.

Waves and Tides

Waves develop when wind, the **tides,** or other events cause water to move. Waves are beneficial to ocean life because many animals rely on them to distribute their food or wash up on shore. Discover the different kinds of waves with Emma and Louis—some of them are really enormous!

Many coastlines are awash with mussels that have been repeatedly "rinsed" by waves. Mussels absorb tiny pieces of food—as well as nitrogen and phosphor—through their **gills,** cleaning the seawater in the process. Sea mussels pump about 1.3 gallons (five liters) of water through their bodies per hour, while oysters can pump up to 6.5 gallons (25 liters) per hour!

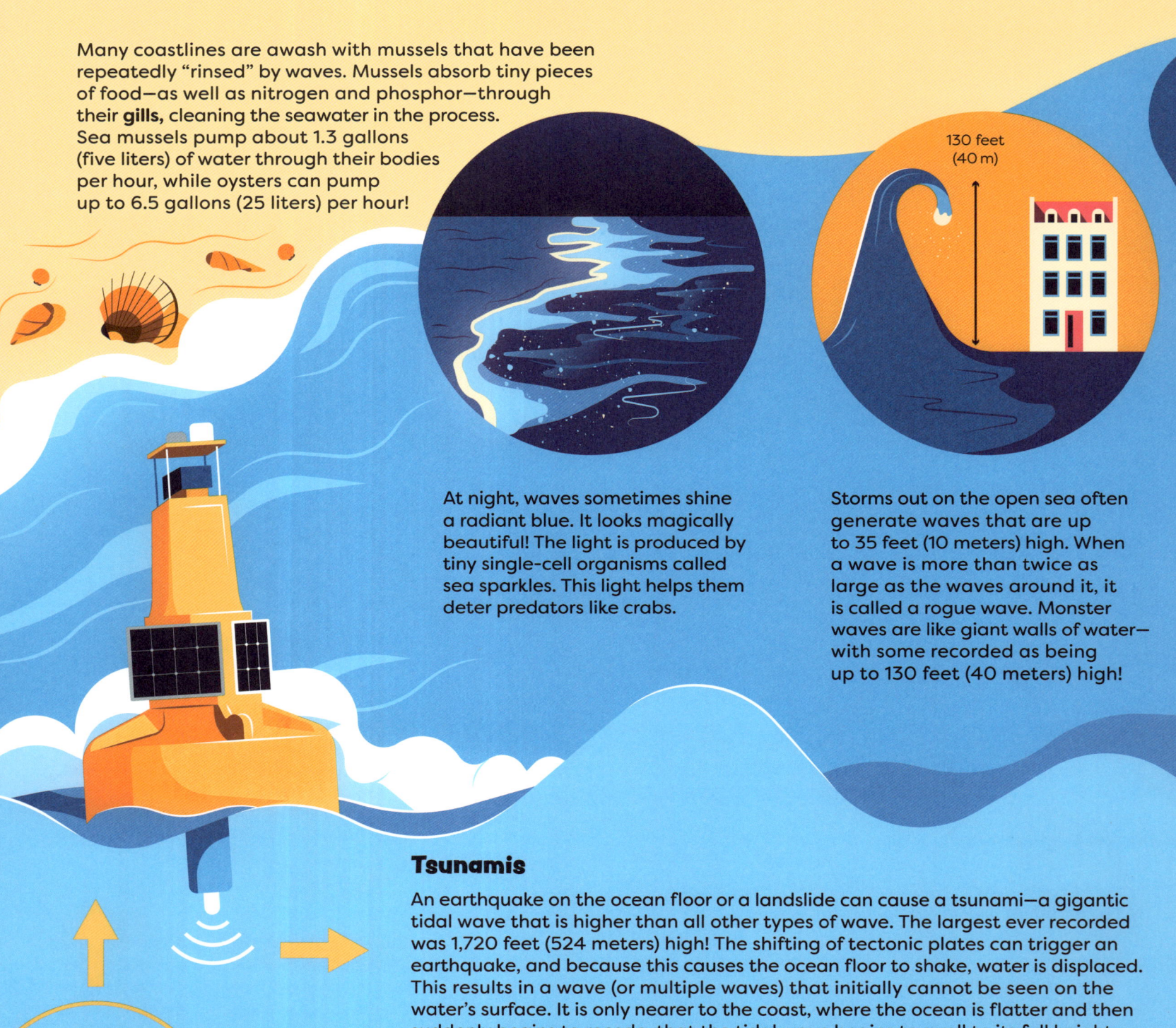

130 feet
(40 m)

At night, waves sometimes shine a radiant blue. It looks magically beautiful! The light is produced by tiny single-cell organisms called sea sparkles. This light helps them deter predators like crabs.

Storms out on the open sea often generate waves that are up to 35 feet (10 meters) high. When a wave is more than twice as large as the waves around it, it is called a rogue wave. Monster waves are like giant walls of water—with some recorded as being up to 130 feet (40 meters) high!

Tsunamis

An earthquake on the ocean floor or a landslide can cause a tsunami—a gigantic tidal wave that is higher than all other types of wave. The largest ever recorded was 1,720 feet (524 meters) high! The shifting of tectonic plates can trigger an earthquake, and because this causes the ocean floor to shake, water is displaced. This results in a wave (or multiple waves) that initially cannot be seen on the water's surface. It is only nearer to the coast, where the ocean is flatter and then suddenly begins to recede, that the tidal wave begins to swell to its full height.

If you want to see how waves form as the result of wind, simply blow on the surface of a puddle. Your breath will create a kind of wind direction and the water will be pushed in that direction. This is exactly how wind affects the ocean.

Surfers love waves, which provide them with endless fun as they glide along on their boards. But waves aren't only a source of fun: they are also important for sea creatures and keeping the oceans healthy.

The highest point of a wave is called the crest. Wave height is measured by sensors attached to offshore oil rigs.

The force generated by the tides is huge—that's why the movement of water is also used to generate electricity.

Ebb and flow

The ebb and flow of the **tides** also influence the movement of the oceans and the formation of waves. Tides are the result of the movement of the Moon—even though it is hundreds of thousands of miles away from the Earth, its **gravitational forces** are still able to affect the water on our planet.

On the side of the Earth that faces the Moon, water is attracted toward it as though it's a magnet. This causes a tidal bulge. On the other side of the Earth, the **centrifugal force** generated by the **Earth's rotation** creates a smaller tidal bulge. As the Earth completes its rotation, the tidal bulge moves along with the moon. This is what leads to the alternation between low and high tides.

Ocean Currents

Ocean currents are like rivers flowing through the ocean, moving enormous amounts of water around the Earth. They are generated by the **Earth's rotation,** winds, and differences in salt content and temperature within the water. The surface of the ocean floor also has an impact on the direction in which they flow.

Ocean currents ensure an exchange of cold and warm water, **oxygen,** and **nutrients** between the oceans. Warm water flows away from the **equator** toward the two poles, while cold water from the polar regions sinks to the ocean floor and then circulates back to the equator. This cyclical process balances out temperatures both in the water and on land.

George Hadley

The English scientist George Hadley was the first to describe the circulation of air around Earth that begins at the equator: The Sun's rays are strongest at the equator. Wind occurs when the Sun heats up the air. The warm air expands and becomes lighter. This causes it to rise to a higher altitude and flow away from the equator. Because it cools on its journey, it descends again around the subtropics and flows back toward the equator near the ground level. These winds are commonly called the trade winds and this circulatory system is known as the Hadley cell.

(EAST) GREENLAND CURRENT

NORTH AMERICA

CALIFORNIA CURRENT

GULF STREAM

NORTH EQUATORIAL CURRENT

SOUTH EQUATORIAL CURRENT

SOUTH AMERICA

BRAZIL CURRENT

HUMBOLDT CURRENT

Not all oceans have the same saltiness! As water flows from the Pacific to the Atlantic (via the Indian Ocean), a good amount of it evaporates. This causes its salt content to increase. The water then flows in the direction of Iceland and Greenland. At 35 parts per thousand, the Atlantic is roughly three grams per liter saltier than the Pacific. The Mediterranean is saltier still, at around 38 parts per thousand, although that's nothing compared to the Dead Sea (which is actually a lake), which has a salt content of 340 parts per thousand.

Oceans are important for the Earth's **climate** because they remove **carbon dioxide (CO_2)** from the atmosphere.

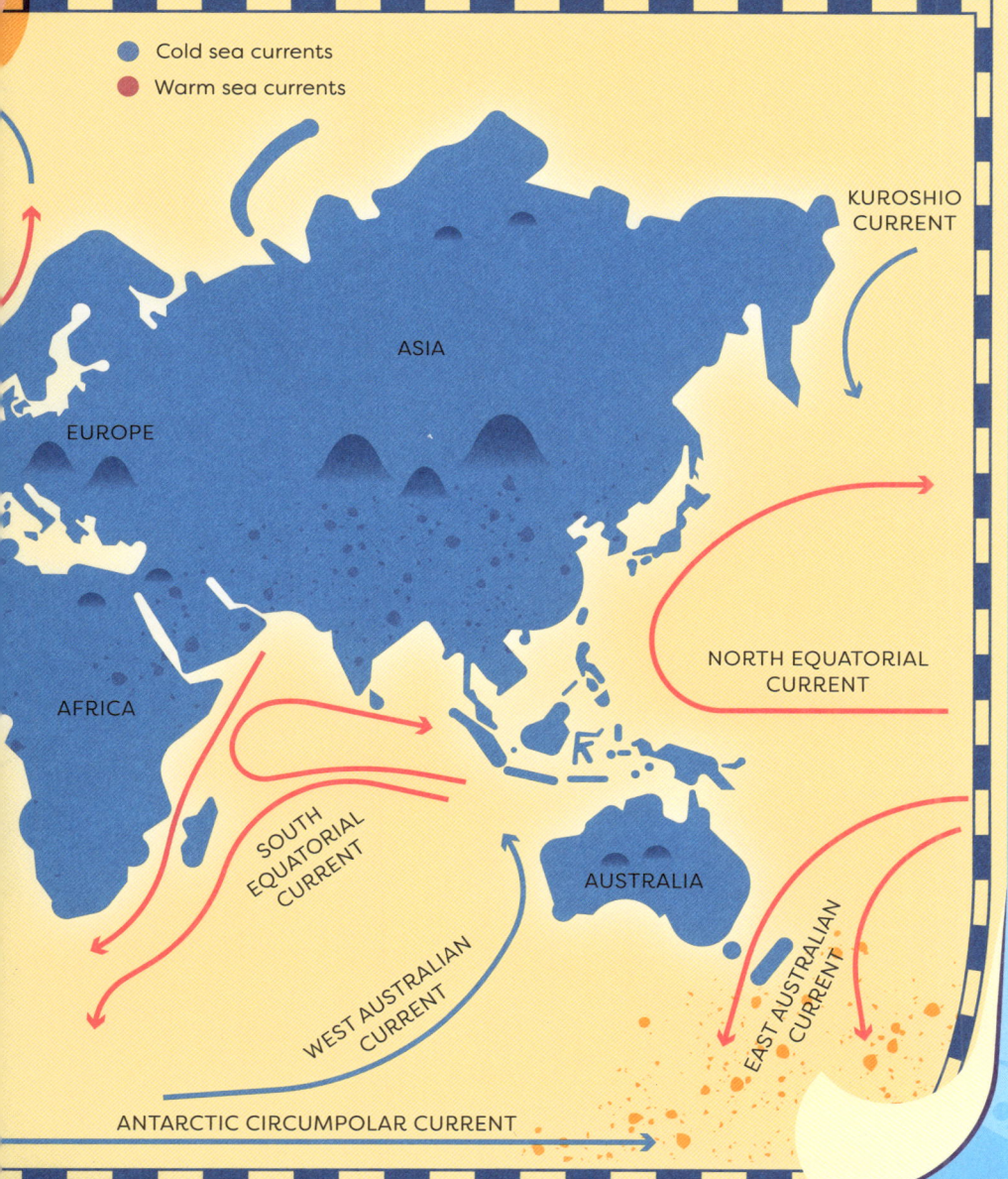

- Cold sea currents
- Warm sea currents

KUROSHIO CURRENT

ASIA

EUROPE

NORTH EQUATORIAL CURRENT

AFRICA

SOUTH EQUATORIAL CURRENT

AUSTRALIA

WEST AUSTRALIAN CURRENT

EAST AUSTRALIAN CURRENT

ANTARCTIC CIRCUMPOLAR CURRENT

The water cycle

The oceans play a major role in our planet's water cycle. The Sun's rays cause water to **evaporate** from the oceans up into the sky, where it condenses to form clouds. Air currents cause these clouds to move around the atmosphere. Eventually, the water contained in the clouds is returned to the Earth's surface (on land as well as at sea) in the form of rain, hail, or snow. This cycle is important for the regulation of the Earth's climate and providing land with water.

The World's Oceans

Two thirds of the Earth is covered by salt water, making up the five oceans and their marginal seas. The largest ocean is the Pacific, while the smallest lies between the Russian and Canadian coasts and is called the Arctic Ocean.

ARCTIC OCEAN

PACIFIC OCEAN

ATLANTIC OCEAN

• Wreck of the Titanic

INDIAN OCEAN

PACIFIC OCEAN

The world's saltwater regions are often called the seven seas. Along with the five oceans, the Atlantic and Pacific are additionally divided into North and South.

SOUTHERN OCEAN

The passenger ship Titanic sank in the Atlantic on April 15, 1912, after colliding with an iceberg. Many people searched for the famous ocean liner's wreck, but it was not found until 1985, at a depth of almost 12,500 feet (3,800 meters). Ever since its sinking, it has been settled by sea sponges, shrimps, and crabs, which have eaten away at the ship's wood. The wreck was inspected with the help of robots, and new species, like the bacteria Halomonas titanicae, have been discovered as a result. Some scientists believe the wreck of the Titanic will have totally disappeared within a few decades.

The Atlantic Ocean

With a surface area of just over 41 million square miles (106 million square kilometers), the Atlantic is the world's second-largest ocean. It formed 150 million years ago, when the supercontinent Pangaea broke up.

Atlantic flyingfish (Cheilopogon melanurus)

These **fish** can leap out of the water and use their wing-like pectoral fins to glide through the air—for up to almost 600 feet (180 meters) at a time!

Bigscale scorpionfish (Scorpaena scrofa)

These fish live at the bottom of the ocean and are an example of what are known as ambush predators: if a small shrimp swims by, for instance, they quickly open their mouths and suck it up in one go. Scorpionfish are quite slow swimmers themselves and tend to push themselves along the ocean floor using their pectoral fins. Their spines are poisonous.

Queen scallop (Aequipecten opercularis)

These aren't fish, but they can swim! Queen scallops live in the North Atlantic. To move, they clap their shells together, pushing water out in the process, which propels them.

The Arctic Ocean

The Arctic Ocean is found far in our planet's north. It is also known as the North Polar Sea or the Arctic Mediterranean Sea and covers just over six million square miles (14 million square kilometers). Most of the ocean's surface lies beneath a thick layer of ice.

Polar bear (Ursus maritimus)

Polar bears are the largest land carnivores in the world. Because the sea ice they call home is continuously receding thanks to **climate change,** they have begun migrating to **habitats** in North America. This has led to them pairing up with local grizzly bears, which has resulted in cappuccino-colored grolar bears.

The Arctic Ocean is located between three continents: North America, Europe, and Asia.

NORTH AMERICA

ASIA

In winter, two thirds of the Arctic Ocean is covered by ice.

NORTH POLE

EUROPE

The water in the Arctic Ocean can be as cold as 25 degrees Fahrenheit (minus-four degrees Celsius).

Many creatures live beneath the ice, such as **algae** and tiny crabs. They get their **nutrients** from the ice. This marks the beginning of the Arctic food chain.

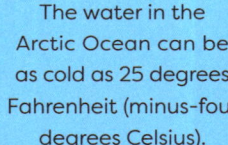

Icebergs

Icebergs are made up of fresh water. They are parts of polar glaciers that have broken off. They can sometimes loom up to over 330 feet (100 meters) above the surface, but what we see are only their peaks: most of an iceberg (up to 90 percent) lies beneath the surface.

Ice floes

Countless ice floes move across the Arctic Ocean—and some of them are really enormous. Ice floes are sheets of frozen sea water (so salt water, unlike icebergs). Wind and waves cause them to stack up on each other like pancakes. Over time, this causes ice sheets to form that are between 33 and 65 feet (10 to 20 meters) thick.

The Indian Ocean

At over 27 million square miles (70 million square kilometers), this is the third-largest ocean on Earth—and also the warmest.

ASIA

AFRICA

Indo-Pacific sailfish (Istiophorus platypterus)

Sailfish can swim at speeds of almost 30 mph (45 km/h). They stun their **prey** by attacking with their long, sharp bills and then eat them in a single bite.

When sailfish want to swim fast, they retract their dorsal fin so that it is pressed flat against their back. This means they encounter less resistance in the water.

Madagascar is the largest island in the Indian Ocean. It is home to many **endemic** (native) plants and animals.

The largest examined giant clam to date weighed 660 pounds (300 kilograms) and was 4.5 feet long (1.4 meters). These mussels are unable to move on their own. They situate themselves on a coral reef and feed on plankton that they filter out of the water.

Leafy seadragon (Phycodurus eques)

These creatures are related to seahorses. Because of their leaf-like extremities, they look a lot like algae. This is a very useful attribute, as it provides them with perfect camouflage while they wait for their prey (such as small crustaceans). This camouflage technique is known as mimesis (imitation of another species).

The Pacific Ocean

The Pacific Ocean is the largest and deepest ocean. It has a surface area of over 62 million square miles (160 million square kilometers).

The Pacific Ocean holds two impressive records. One, it has a surface area that is larger than all of the Earth's continents combined. And two, if you include the surface areas of its marginal seas, it is almost as large as all of the other oceans and seas put together. It really is rather vast! The Pacific holds over half of the Earth's open water supply.

NORTH AMERICA

PACIFIC OCEAN

There are over 400 active volcanoes along the Pacific Plate. This chain of volcanoes is called the Pacific Ring of Fire.

ASIA

AUSTRALIA

Seahorses are incredibly good parents: when they mate, the female seahorse lays hundreds of eggs in the male's brood pouch, where the eggs develop until they are ready to hatch.

Giant Pacific octopus (Enteroctopus dofleini)

Octopuses are a subspecies of cephalopods. Each of a giant octopus's arms is equipped with up to 250 suction cups, which can be as large as saucers. Giant octopuses live in caves and can squeeze their bodies through the smallest of crevices. Their beaks look similar to those of parrots and they use them to bite through the shells of crabs. Their saliva is poisonous.

Giant octopuses mate only once in their lives. After the female has laid up to 100,000 eggs, she stops eating for six and a half months. She dedicates herself to looking after her eggs and then she dies.

The Southern Ocean

Also known as the Antarctic Ocean, this ocean surrounds the continent of Antarctica, which is almost entirely covered with ice.

ANTARCTICA

Antarctic krill (Euphausiacea)

These tiny shrimp-like creatures live in the Southern Ocean, where they feed on **algae** and **plankton** that they filter out of the water. They are known as krill and can grow to be up to 2.7 inches (68 millimeters) long. Researchers have found them in concentrations of between 10,000 and 30,000 per cubic meter and estimate that up to 500 million metric tons of krill live in the Southern Ocean.

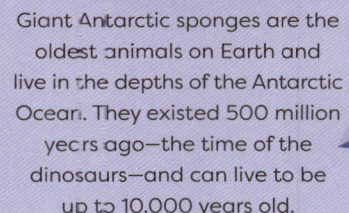

Giant Antarctic sponges are the oldest animals on Earth and live in the depths of the Antarctic Ocean. They existed 500 million years ago—the time of the dinosaurs—and can live to be up to 10,000 years old.

Krill is a key component of the food chain. They serve as food for whales, seals, and birds.

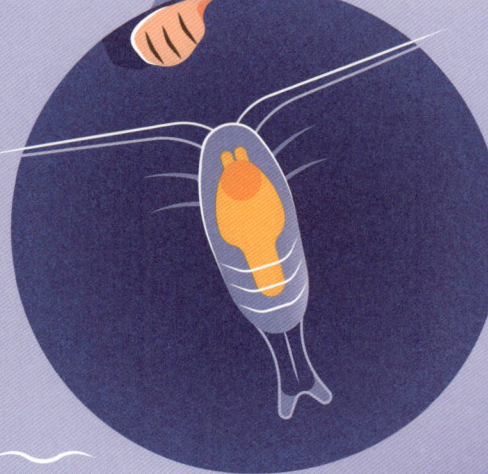

Plankton in the Southern Ocean store **carbon dioxide** that they draw from the atmosphere.

Emperor penguin (Aptenodytes forsteri)

With this species of penguin, the male **incubates** the eggs while the female hunts **fish** and squid beneath the ice. To protect themselves against the Antarctic's extreme cold, these **birds** huddle together in extremely tightly packed groupings of up to 5,000. They regularly change places, so that they all get to be in the center of the **colony.**

Algae and Plants

The oceans are filled with billions of **algae.** They serve as food for many aquatic creatures—and are essential for the survival of humans and animals as a whole, because they produce **oxygen,** which we need to breathe.

Giant kelp (Macrocystis pyrifera)

The West Coast of North America is populated by immeasurably large kelp forests. These vast swathes of brown algae are home to numerous **invertebrates** (such as squid) and many different **fish** species, as well as **mammals** such as sea otters. Giant kelp is one of the fastest-growing organisms on the planet (growing up to 24 inches (60 centimeters) per day) and can reach a length of up to 200 feet (60 meters).

No other animal has fur as thick as that of a sea otter. When underwater they can blow air into their fur to provide extra insulation against the cold. Sea otters eat about a quarter of their body weight in food each day.

Kelp forests serve as sheltered spaces for sea creatures. Cat sharks, for example, attach their eggs to giant kelp strands. Over nine months, a baby shark develops inside them. Because the eggs' casings have such a peculiar form, they are also sometimes called mermaid's purses.

Algae, seagrass, and giant kelp all perform photosynthesis. That means they transform carbon dioxide into oxygen. Almost all the oxygen in the air, which we humans need to breathe, is created through photosynthesis. Aquatic plants and algae are also important for the Earth's climate, because they can store carbon dioxide for long periods of time. When a plant dies, it sinks to the ocean floor, meaning that the carbon dioxide stored within it will not be released back into the atmosphere for a long time.

Algae are among our planet's oldest organisms—they have existed for over 500 million years!

Microalgae

Microalgae cannot be seen with the naked eye, but that doesn't mean they aren't super-important. These tiny plants—phytoplankton—are the first link in the ocean's food chain. This means that the existence of all other sea creatures is dependent on these algae. One example of microalgae is Chlamydomonas reinhardtii (a green form of algae).

Giants and Pipsqueaks

The blue whale is so huge it's impossible to ignore. But there are other ocean creatures that cannot be seen with the naked eye. They are often only a single cell. Come along as Emma and Louis encounter the smallest and largest creatures of the ocean!

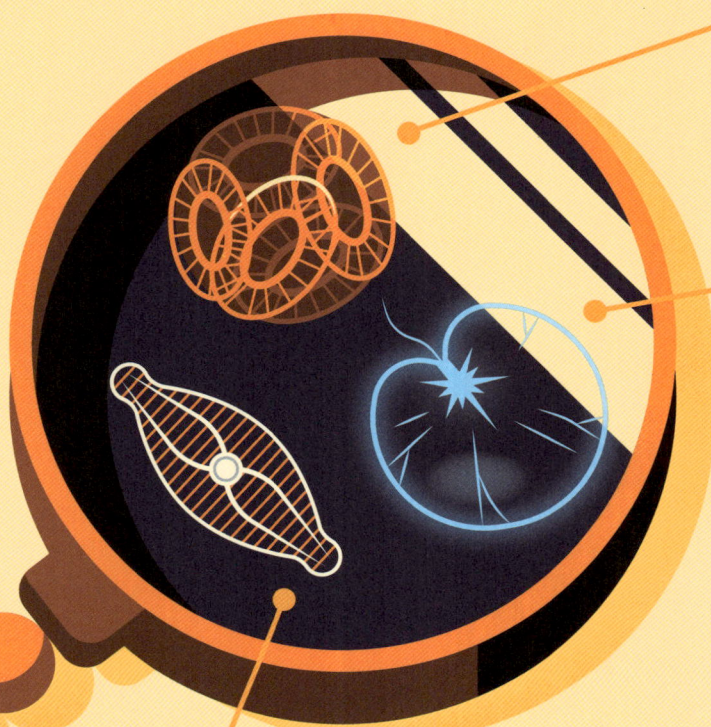

Calcite algae (Haptophyta)

These **algae** are smaller than a grain of salt. The single-cell organisms build up a crust in order to protect themselves. More than 100 million of these tiny creatures can be found in just 0.2 gallons (one liter) of seawater. Imagine, then, how many there must be in the oceans as a whole!

Sea sparkles (Noctiluca miliaris)

Sea sparkles can be observed from the beach at night. These single-cell organisms emit light through the movement of the waves or when they are otherwise disturbed. This helps them scare away predators such as crabs.

A human body is made up of about 75 trillion cells, while calcite algae, for example, consist of only a single cell! Algae come in many different colors, by the way, such as green, brown, and red.

With a size of up to eight inches (20 centimeters), the dwarf lanternshark is the smallest predatory fish in the ocean.

Silica algae (Diatoms)

Silica algae are very important for our planet, because they produce around a third of Earth's **oxygen.** There are about 6,000 different species of silica algae. A component of **plankton,** they provide key **nutrients** for a countless number of sea creatures.

Giant siphonophore (Praya dubia)

This species actually exists in colonies composed of millions of tiny **zooids** that together form a single body. Each zooid in the **colony** has a special task to carry out. There are some specimens that look like illuminated spirals and whose **tentacles** can be over 130 feet (40 meters) long.

Leatherback sea turtle (Dermochelys coriacea)

Measuring up to around six feet (two meters) long, this species is the largest sea turtle. They have a thick skin and can weigh up to 1,500 pounds (700 kilograms).

Ocean sunfish (Mola mola)

This species of **fish** somewhat resembles the Sun in terms of shape. It can weigh over 4,400 pounds (2,000 kilograms)—almost as much as a hippopotamus! Sunfish live in the open ocean, sometimes at depths of over 1,600 feet (500 meters).

Giant oceanic manta ray (Mobula birostris)

These rays can grow to be up to 29.5 feet (nine meters) long and weigh up to three tons! They have strong fins, with a wing-span of up to 22.9 feet (seven meters), which means they are able to fend off attacks from sharks and orcas.

Whale shark (Rhincodon typus)

The world's longest fish feed on very small creatures, filtering out crustaceans and shrimps from the water and growing to be up to 46 feet (14 meters) long. Their skin is thicker than any other animal's (almost four inches, or 10 centimeters) and they have huge mouths that are almost 60 inches (1.5 meters) wide. Would you be able to fit inside?

Blue whale (Balaenoptera musculus)

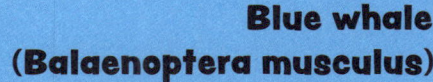

The blue whale is the world's largest **mammal** and the largest creature that has ever lived on Earth. They can grow to be almost 110 feet (33 meters) long. They also hold another impressive record: their hearts beat at a rate of only six to eight times a minute, which is the world's slowest heartbeat.

Predators

Careful, it's not only sharp teeth that are dangerous! The oceans are filled with many ingenious predators. Some attack quickly, while others use clever tricks to snare their **prey**.

Great white shark (Carcharodon carcharias)

These sharks' teeth are triangular in shape and so sharp that they can tear their prey in half with a single bite. If one of their teeth falls out, another moves forward to take its place. All species of shark have multiple layers of teeth that grow along their jaws and can regenerate if necessary.

Red lionfish (Pterois volitans)

The red lionfish first stalks its prey, then quickly opens its mouth to suck it up in one go. The suction force it creates gives the prey no chance of escape.

Because they can regrow (or "reload") their teeth if they fall out or are damaged, sharks are said to have a "revolver bite."

Green moray eel (Gymnothorax funebris)

The thick layer of slime that coats these eels' skin gives them a green appearance. This allows them to camouflage themselves well within the crevices of rocks. They identify their prey using smell and then dash out, lightning-quick, from their hiding place to attack them with their pointy teeth. Green moray eels can grow to be over eight feet (2.5 meters) long.

Sperm whale (Physeter macrocephalus)

These enormous **whales** can dive down to great depths and hunt giant squid. They often bear scars on their skin that result from these underwater battles.

Peacock mantis shrimp (Odontodactylus scyllarus)

These small crustaceans have a unique hunting style: they use their club-shaped forelegs to smash the shells of sea snails. The speed at which they do this makes it one of the fastest movements observed in the animal kingdom.

Orca whale (Orcinus orca)

Orca whales are also known as killer whales. These intelligent predators feed on penguins as well as other aquatic **mammals** such as dolphins and seals. They hunt in packs and communicate by whistling to each other. This means they are even able to prey upon great white sharks or baleen whales—which are larger than they are.

Sea lamprey (Petromyzon marinus)

These **fish,** also known as vampire fish, have suction cups for mouths that contain teeth. They even have teeth on their tongues, which help to pierce the skin of other fish, because it's their blood they want suck out.

Fish

Fish have existed for over 500 million years. They were the first animal to develop an internal skeleton—and there is such an incredible variety of them, ranging from the puffer fish to the primitive coelacanth.

How do fish breathe?

Water contains **oxygen** that fish filter out using their **gills**, which are composed of fine layers of skin. These layers contain small blood vessels called capillaries. As the water runs over the gills the capillaries pick up the oxygen that's in it and this is then transported round the fish's body. Their gills also allow fish to expel **carbon dioxide.** Water must constantly be flowing through their gills for fish to get enough oxygen to survive.

Inhaling

Exhaling

Most fish have gill covers that are always in motion so that new water can enter their gills. However, some fish, like mako sharks and blue sharks, do not have gill covers. Because of this their bodies must always be in motion so that water keeps flowing through their gills. This is why they always keep their mouths open while they are swimming.

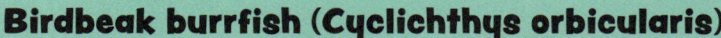

Frilled shark (Chlamydoselachus anguineus)

Their gill slits and their wide mouths, which take up half of their entire heads, make frilled sharks look like creatures from the time of the dinosaurs. Researchers say that they existed 95 million years ago—that's why they are also called living fossils.

Birdbeak burrfish (Cyclichthys orbicularis)

These fish suck up large quantities of water in order to be able to inflate their bodies and erect their barbs to protect themselves against hungry predators. They have a beak-like mouth that they can use to break open sea urchins—whose barbs don't scare them in the slightest.

Remora (Echeneidae)

These fish are very clever indeed: they have a kind of suction cup on their backs that allows them to attach themselves to other fish, turtles, or **whales** and be carried along as they move. Sometimes they also try their luck getting a free ride with divers or even ships! That's why they are sometimes also called suckerfish.

Scalloped hammerhead (Sphyrna lewini)

These sharks' eyes and nostrils are located on the outer tips of their heads. Sometimes they ram into each other to communicate. This is not always a friendly gesture, however, as they also do this to threaten each other.

Greenland shark (Somniosus microcephalus)

This species can live to be incredibly old: researchers have discovered a specimen that has been alive for 400 years! They can weigh up to a ton, grow to be almost 20 feet (six meters) long, and are good at withstanding the cold. The water in the Arctic Ocean is around 32 degrees Fahrenheit (zero degrees Celsius).

West Indian Ocean coelacanth (Latimeria chalumnae)

These creatures have been around for over 360 million years, which means they existed at the same time as the dinosaurs! Until around 100 years ago, it was thought that they were extinct. Because they are largely found at great depths, they can only be observed from submarines.

Because they don't have eyelids, fish sleep with their eyes open. Some, like the whiptail stingray, like to burrow down in the sand when they need to rest.

Invertebrates

As different as worms, jellyfish, and octopuses may appear, they do have one thing in common: none of them have internal skeletons. This is why they are called **invertebrates**.

Common fish louse (Argulus foliaceus)

These tiny parasites attach themselves to **fish** and suck their blood. They use their legs to swim when searching for a new host.

Textile cone (Conus textile)

These sea snails can grow to be up to six inches (15 centimeters) long and have a very distinct shell. Their beautiful appearance is deceptive, however, as they are anything but harmless. Textile cones have a hunting weapon that resembles a harpoon and delivers poison to their victims. This allows these snails to paralyze worms, other snails, and even fish that they then swallow whole. Their poison is also harmful to humans.

Common cuttlefish (Sepia officinalis)

The most intelligent mollusks in the ocean, cuttlefish are able to adapt to their environment, use tools, and even count. They also have very good memories and are able to remember things for their entire lives.

Greater blue-ringed octopus (Hapalochlaena lunulata)

Only about four inches (10 centimeters) long, these are among the deadliest animals in the world when they bite. Their venom is produced by **bacteria** that live within them. When they feel threatened, the blue rings on their bodies start to flash.

Pacific sea nettle
(Chrysaora fuscescens)

These jellyfish use their nettles (or nematocysts) to paralyze their **prey** and then pull them into their body using their **tentacles,** where they then digest them.

Australian box jelly
(Chironex fleckeri)

Also known as sea wasps, their 60 tentacles make these creatures some of the most dangerous that roam the ocean. Their venomous stinging cells can even prove fatal to humans.

Jellyfish have no brains, only a basic digestive system, and a fascinating life cycle. An adult jellyfish is called a medusa. They lay eggs that then develop into larvae. These transform into polyps, which firmly attach themselves to a solid surface. The polyps eventually split off a part of themselves, which then becomes a separate larva that drifts away from the original polyp and ultimately develops into a medusa.

European lobster
(Homarus gammarus)

Lobsters usually have one pincer that's larger than the other. The larger, "crusher" pincer is used to smash open other creatures' shells, while the smaller, "cutter" pincer is used to grab and dissect their prey. They wait patiently for their victims in rocks' crevices. European lobsters can grow to be over three feet (one meter) long. If they lose one of their legs, antennae, or pincers, they simply grow back.

Acorn barnacle
(Balanus glandula)

Although these barnacles look like mussels, they are actually small crustaceans that live on rocks. Acorn barnacles use their legs to filter the **nutrients** they need out of the water. They are protected by a shell made of calcite.

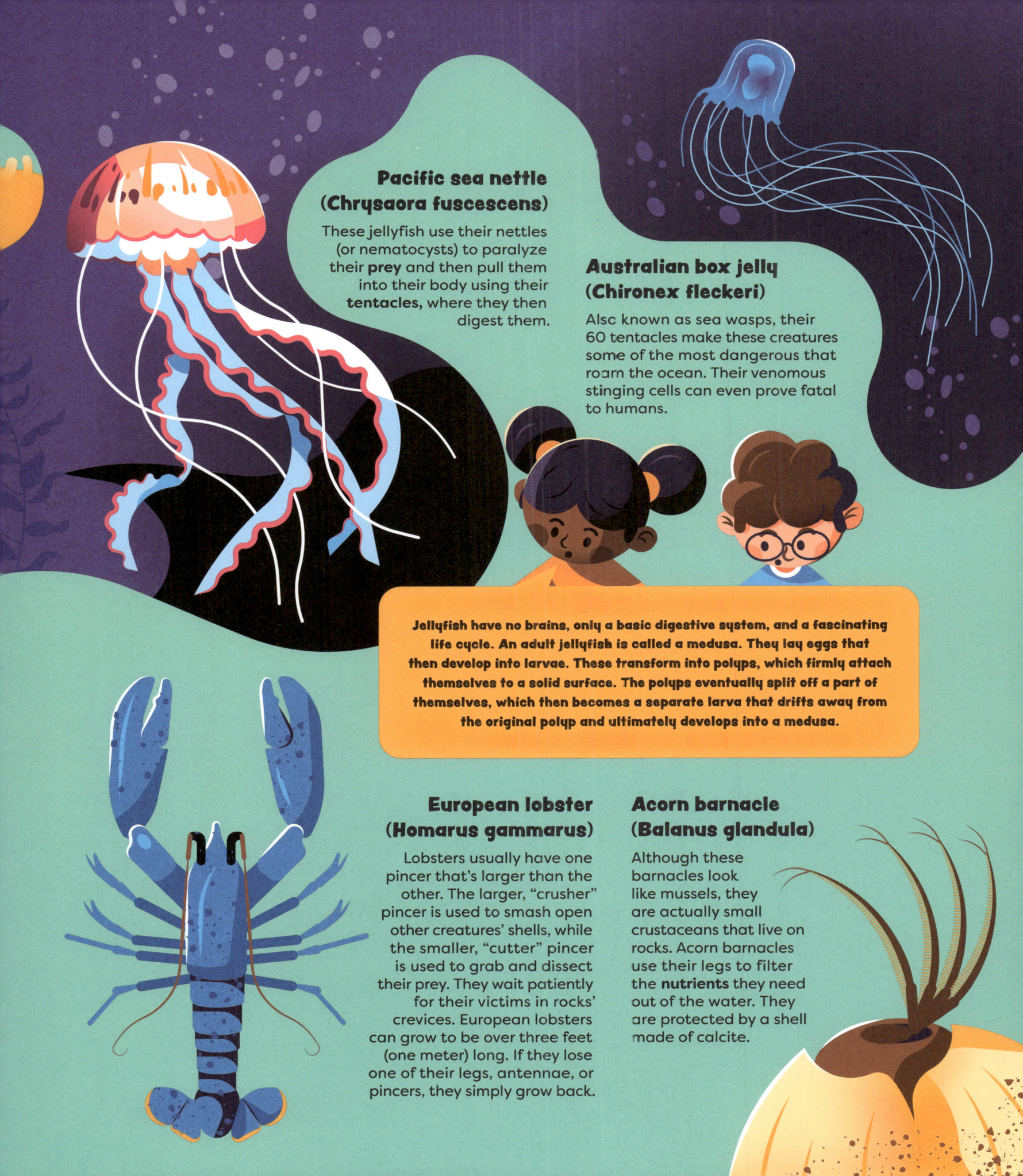

Mammals

Mammals have existed on Earth for around 220 million years. They are **vertebrates** (meaning they have an internal skeleton) and all have one thing in common: they nurse their young with milk—including those that live underwater!

Blue whale (Balaenoptera musculus)

Blue whales are baleen whales, which means they have a hair-like structure (baleen) on their upper jaw that they use to filter krill out of the water. Their stomachs are capable of holding up to around two tons of krill at a time. Blue whales themselves can weigh up to 190 tons—as much as 30 elephants, 225 cows, or 2,500 humans. Their calls can be up to 180 decibels loud, which is noisier than a jet plane. This allows them to communicate with fellow blue whales that are more than a thousand miles away.

How do mammals in the ocean sleep and breathe?

In order to survive, dolphins and **whales** must regularly return to the water's surface for air. For them, breathing is a conscious action, unlike with us humans. We breathe automatically. Whales and dolphins remind themselves to come up for air and to breathe. This is why, at night, half of their brain stays awake while the other half switches off—with each half alternating responsibility each night.

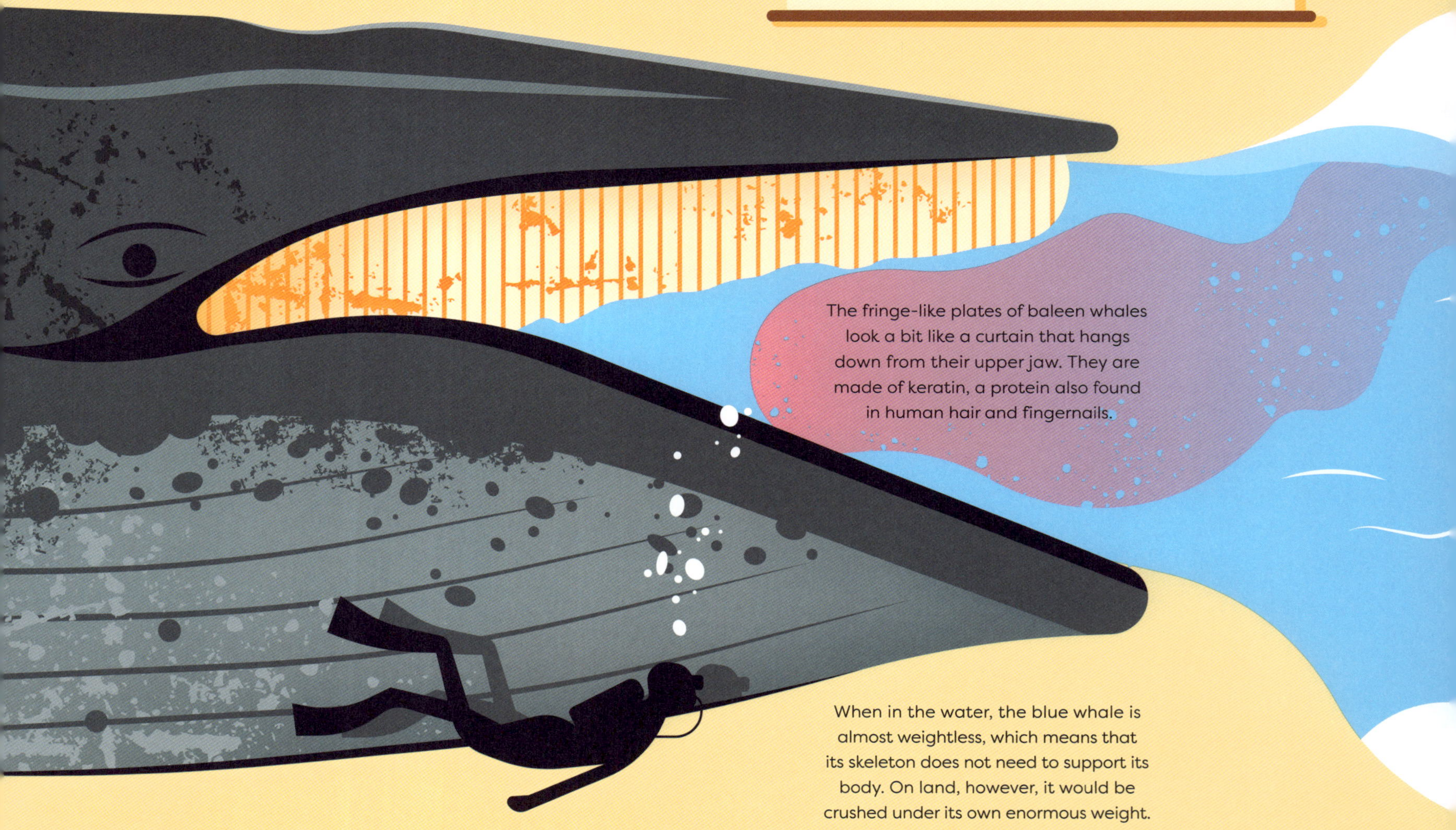

The fringe-like plates of baleen whales look a bit like a curtain that hangs down from their upper jaw. They are made of keratin, a protein also found in human hair and fingernails.

When in the water, the blue whale is almost weightless, which means that its skeleton does not need to support its body. On land, however, it would be crushed under its own enormous weight.

Common bottlenose dolphin (Tursiops truncatus)

These dolphins are some of the cleverest mammals around. Every bottlenose dolphin has its own distinct whistle that its peers learn to recognize. They use these sounds to address each other and communicate. Dolphins hunt squid or salmon in packs and use ultrasound waves to work in harmony with each other.

Spade-toothed whale (Mesoplodon traversii)

Little is known about these creatures. They are the least-researched **whale** species in the ocean. To this day, no living specimen has been observed in the water. Everything we know about this species comes from their dead bodies that have washed up on land.

Hooded seal (Cystophora cristata)

In order to impress females or to scare off other males, male hooded seals inflate a bladder on their heads, which makes them look like big balloons!

When humans jump into water, some pinch their nostrils closed with their fingers so that no water can get in. When a sea lion's facial muscles are relaxed, their nostrils are naturally sealed. If they want to breathe, they must tense these same muscles to inhale air. This means no water enters their noses when they are submerged.

California sea lion (Zalophus californianus)

These creatures are intelligent hunters that can dive to a depth of almost 100 feet (30 meters) and hold their breath for up to 10 minutes. Their whiskers allow them to detect their **prey** in dark or murky waters. Sea lions have a thick layer of blubber (fat) that helps keep them warm.

Birds and Reptiles

The oceans are filled with many fascinating **fish** and **mammals,** but also many **reptiles** and **birds** make them their home. Check out some of the ones that Emma and Louis have encountered!

Magnificent frigatebird (Fregata magnificens)

Males of this species have a striking red gular sac (throat skin) that they inflate to attract females. Frigatebirds can be over three feet (one meter) long, have a wingspan of over six feet (two meters), and sustain themselves with squid and fish that they pluck out of the water while in flight.

Marine iguana (Amblyrhynchus cristatus)

Marine iguanas live on the rocky coastlines of the Galápagos Islands. They can grow to be almost five feet (1.5 meters) in size. They are masters of survival and feed upon **algae** that they scrape off the rocks. If one of their teeth falls out, another simply grows in its place.

Atlantic ridley sea turtle (Lepidochelys kempii)

At only 27 inches (70 centimeters) long, these are the smallest of all sea turtles. They are also known as Kemp's ridley sea turtles, named after the US fisherman Richard M. Kemp, who was the first to identify them as a distinct species.

Blue-footed booby (Sula nebouxii)

To impress females, male blue-footed boobies perform a dance during which they alternate the raising of their feet. The more radiant the blue of their feet the better, as this signals to females that their potential suitor is strong and healthy! If a female is interested in the male, they begin dancing together. These birds live together in large groups.

Leatherback sea turtles get their name from their leathery, oily skin, which helps protect them from predators. The grow to be between six and 10 feet (two to three meters) long and are the largest sea turtles in the world. Another record they hold is they can swim almost 4,000 feet (1,200 meters) deep! They feed on plankton and jellyfish, and are immune to the latter's venom. If sea turtles didn't feed on jellyfish, and thus limit their numbers, the amount of them in the ocean would be damaging to certain habitats.

Turtles lay eggs to reproduce, but these eggs need warmth in order to develop and hatch. For this reason, turtles bring them onto land, where they bury them in sand that gets heat from the Sun. When temperatures exceed 85 degrees Fahrenheit (or more precisely, 29.9 degrees Celsius), the eggs hatch into female turtles, whereas if it's colder, they hatch into males.

Ocean Migration

Many animals roam the oceans in search of food and to raise their young. Some species travel distances of over 6,000 miles (10,000 kilometers) and back!

Most species of **whale** spend their summers in the Southern or Arctic oceans, where they consume enormous amounts of krill in order to develop a thick layer of blubber. A gray whale calf, for instance, will put on around 65 pounds (30 kilograms) of weight per day.

Whales don't navigate through the oceans using their eyes, but rather by using **echolocation** to sense the position of coastlines, underwater mountains, and canyons.

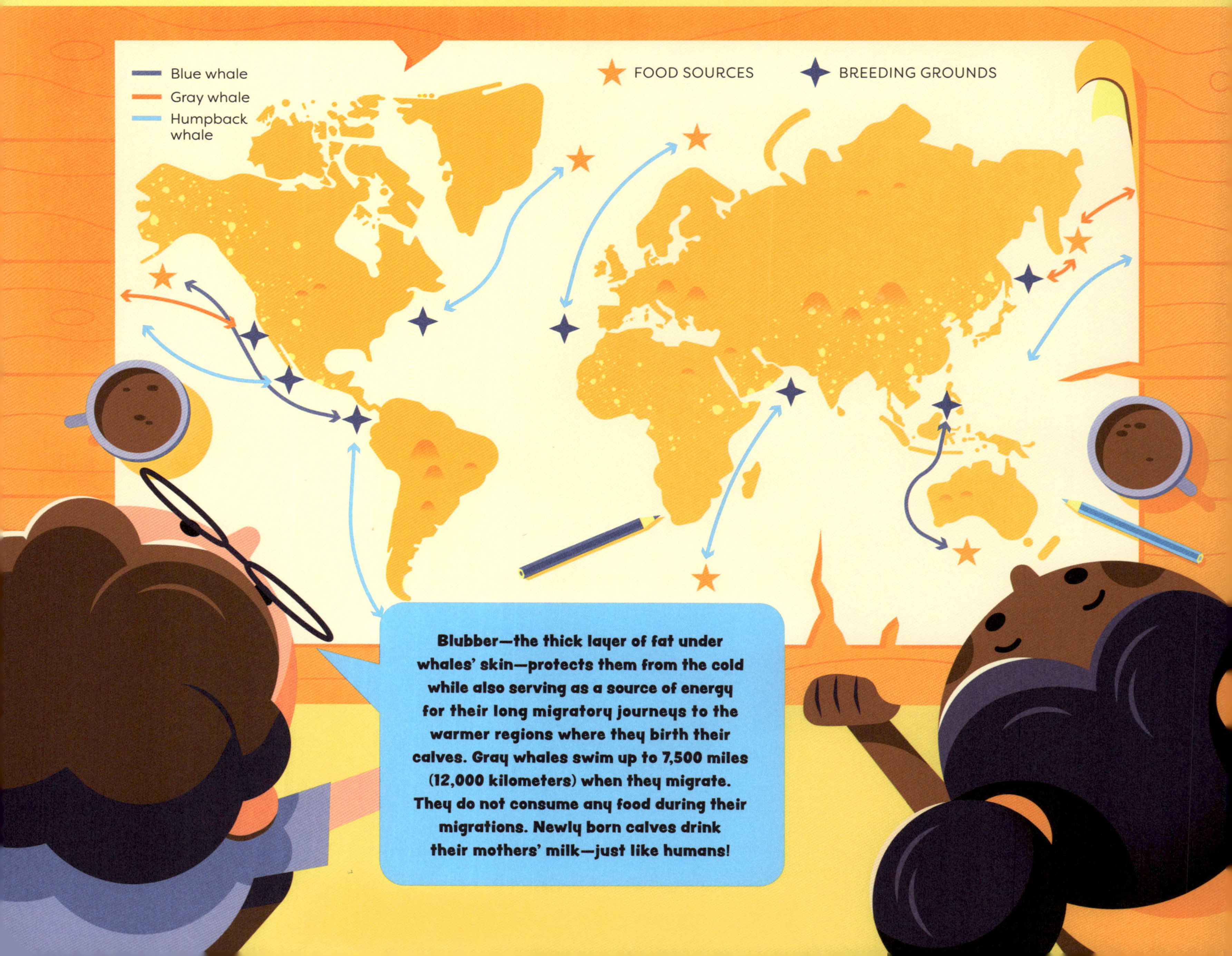

— Blue whale
— Gray whale
— Humpback whale

★ FOOD SOURCES   ◆ BREEDING GROUNDS

Blubber—the thick layer of fat under whales' skin—protects them from the cold while also serving as a source of energy for their long migratory journeys to the warmer regions where they birth their calves. Gray whales swim up to 7,500 miles (12,000 kilometers) when they migrate. They do not consume any food during their migrations. Newly born calves drink their mothers' milk—just like humans!

The Arctic tern breeds in the Arctic in summer and then flies all the way to the Antarctic Ocean in winter. They have the longest migratory path of all **birds,** traveling a distance of almost 20,000 miles (32,000 kilometers) there and back.

Some animals, such as sea turtles, navigate using wave patterns that develop near coastlines or islands. They also orient themselves according to currents and variations in water temperature. Through these processes, they are even able to find the very same beach on which they emerged from their own shells as hatchlings.

Green sea turtles use the Earth's magnetic field to return to their original breeding grounds.

Leatherback turtles swim over 4,300 miles (7,000 kilometers) to get from their feeding grounds in the ocean to the beaches where they lay their eggs.

Salmon (Salmoninae)

During their lives, salmon swim thousands of miles, changing their **habitats** several times in the process: from the rivers (fresh water) in which they hatch to the ocean (salt water) and then back to the rivers from which they came. They stay in the ocean for up to four years. During this time they eat large quantities of food and grow in size. They then return to their "home" rivers (known as their spawning grounds) to begin the reproductive cycle again.

Coral Reefs

Coral reefs are formed by colonies of stony coral **polyps** that produce exoskeletons made of calcium carbonate. New coral is then able to grow upon these structures. Although these creatures—in all their many forms and colors—appear to be plants, they are in fact animals.

Great Barrier Reef

This reef, just off the coast of Australia, is the largest coral reef on Earth, with a length of 1,400 miles (2,300 kilometers) and covering an area of around 133,000 square miles (almost 345,000 square kilometers). This makes it almost as large as Germany! The Great Barrier Reef is home to an extremely diverse number of species—with 30 **whale** species found there alone, the largest of which is the humpback whale.

Coral reefs provide fish, turtles, sea snails, starfish, sea urchins, shrimps, crabs, and sea sponges with sheltered habitats.

NEW CALEDONIA BARRIER REEF

AUSTRALIA

GREAT BARRIER REEF

Yellow tang change their eye color depending on their mood, from bright (when relaxed) to dark (when frightened or angry).

New Caledonia barrier reef

The New Caledonia barrier reef encloses an area of 9,300 square miles (24,000 square kilometers). It is home to many marine species that live nowhere else on Earth, such as dugongs. These **mammals** are related to elephants.

Sea anemones are "flower animals" that are related to coral.

Each coral polyp consists of a stomach and a mouth, which is surrounded by a ring of tentacles. Around 5,000 species of coral have been discovered so far. There are even coral species that grow at depths of up to 1.25 miles (2,000 meters), where it is really cold!

The coral grouper is an inhabitant of tropical coral reefs.

Bluestripe snappers live together in large shoals.

Grooved brain coral (Diploria labyrinthiformis)

This coral species can grow to have a diameter of up to over 6.5 feet (two meters) and are composed of thousands of tightly connected polyps.

Sea fan (Gorgonia ventalina)

Although they have a net-like appearance, these are in fact a species of coral. Their form depends on whether they grow in shallow water (making them wide and stretched) or in deep water (making them tall). Dolphins use them as a kind of first aid kit, rubbing up against them to take advantage of their antibacterial quality.

Like all reef-forming coral species, the skeletons of mushroom-shaped corals called Ctenactis echinata are formed from minerals found in the ocean.

Where Ocean Meets Land

The areas where ocean and land meet are their own unique worlds. Come along as Emma and Louis discover large crabs, roots that breathe, and sea cows—and learn about how important coastlines are for the Earth's **climate.**

According to the United Nations Environment Programme, seagrass meadows cover over 115,000 square miles (300,000 square kilometers) of seabed.

Seagrass meadows

Giant seagrass meadows can be found along many coastlines around the world. They can be thought of as being a bit like kindergartens for many ocean creatures. They are also hotbeds of diversity: up to one million different species can be found within 100 acres (one hectare) of seagrass meadow.

There is a giant seagrass ecosystem to be found near the islands of the Bahamas. It's around 56,000 square miles (90,000 square kilometers), which is roughly as large as Portugal.

Seagrass meadows help protect coastlines from erosion—which is when they slowly degrade as a result of water currents and winds.

Seagrass meadows also play an important role in terms of the Earth's climate: a single hectare of seagrass meadow stores as much **carbon dioxide** as 10 hectares of forest.

Sea cows (Sirenia)

Sea cows and green sea turtles feed on seagrass. Bonnet sharks (Sphyrna tiburo) also like to graze on seagrass, as do squid, which are in turn a tasty treat for bonnet sharks.

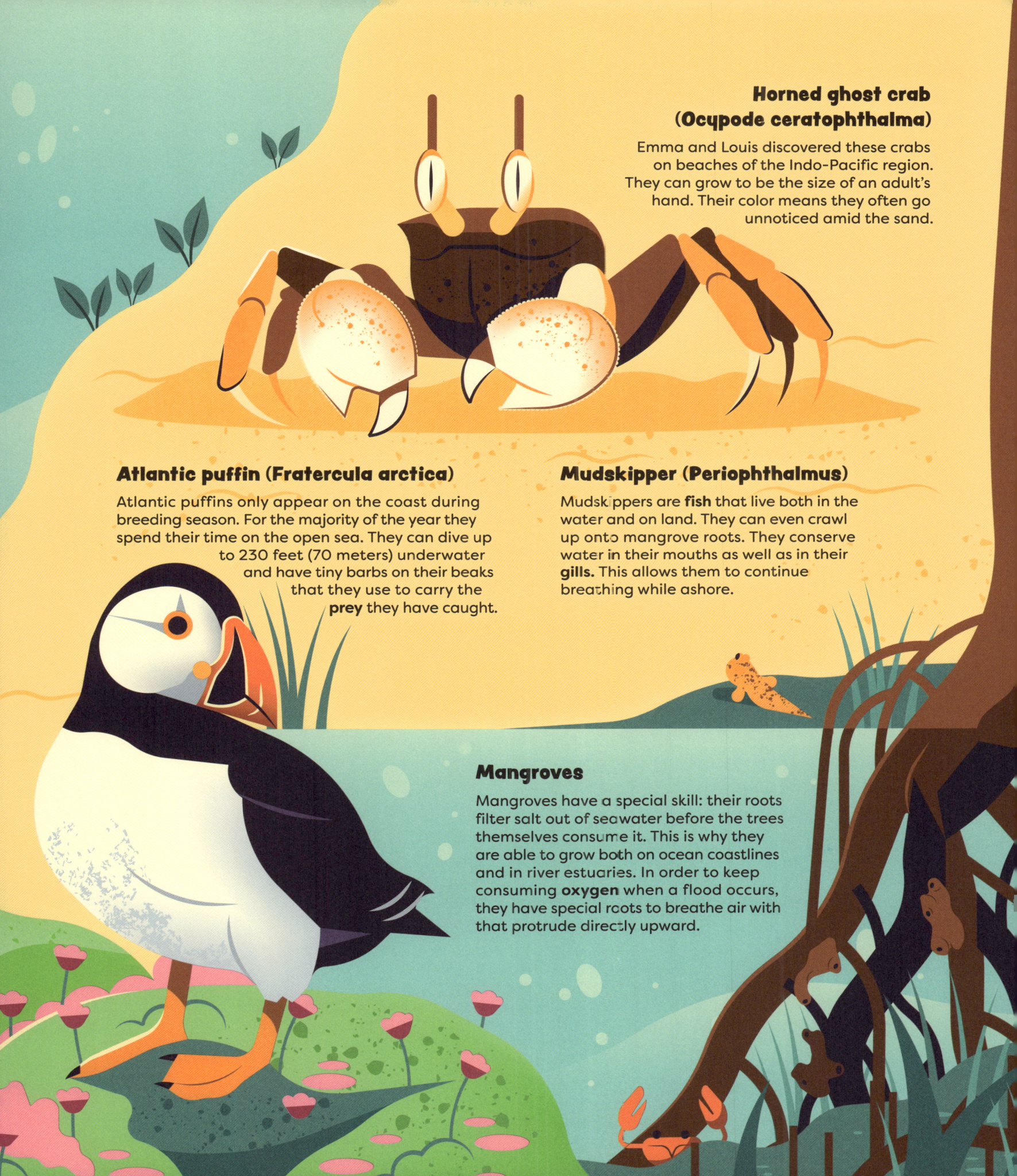

Horned ghost crab (Ocypode ceratophthalma)

Emma and Louis discovered these crabs on beaches of the Indo-Pacific region. They can grow to be the size of an adult's hand. Their color means they often go unnoticed amid the sand.

Atlantic puffin (Fratercula arctica)

Atlantic puffins only appear on the coast during breeding season. For the majority of the year they spend their time on the open sea. They can dive up to 230 feet (70 meters) underwater and have tiny barbs on their beaks that they use to carry the **prey** they have caught.

Mudskipper (Periophthalmus)

Mudskippers are **fish** that live both in the water and on land. They can even crawl up onto mangrove roots. They conserve water in their mouths as well as in their **gills.** This allows them to continue breathing while ashore.

Mangroves

Mangroves have a special skill: their roots filter salt out of seawater before the trees themselves consume it. This is why they are able to grow both on ocean coastlines and in river estuaries. In order to keep consuming **oxygen** when a flood occurs, they have special roots to breathe air with that protrude directly upward.

Underwater Landscapes

Dry land is not the only place you can find landscapes with mountains, valleys, and hills—Emma and Louis have discovered giant mountain ranges and other astounding geological features underwater too!

Seamount

A seamount is an underwater mountain that can rise between around 3,300 feet (1,000 meters) and 13,000 feet (4,000 meters) from the ocean floor without reaching the water's surface. It is estimated that there are between 30,000 and 100,000 seamounts distributed across the Earth's oceans.

The longest mountain range in the world is underwater. The Mid-Atlantic Ridge stretches from the Atlantic to the Arctic Ocean and is four times longer than the Andes, the Rocky Mountains, and the Himalayas all put together.

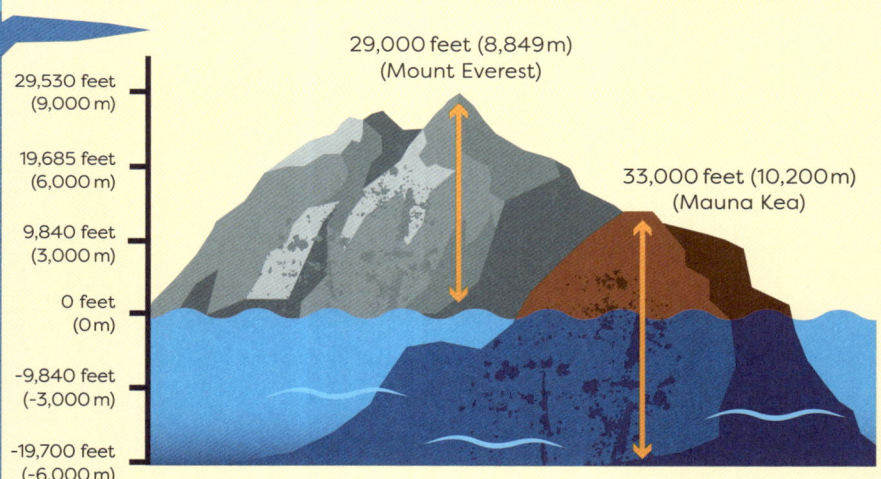

29,000 feet (8,849m)
(Mount Everest)

33,000 feet (10,200m)
(Mauna Kea)

29,530 feet
(9,000 m)

19,685 feet
(6,000 m)

9,840 feet
(3,000 m)

0 feet
(0 m)

-9,840 feet
(-3,000 m)

-19,700 feet
(-6,000 m)

Records

At 29,000 feet (8,849 meters), Mount Everest is often believed to hold the record for being the highest mountain on Earth. But there are two others that surpass it: the volcanoes Mauna Loa and Mauna Kea, on Hawai'i. If measured from sea level, they are "only" 13,000 feet (4,200 meters) high—but measured from the ocean floor, they are almost 33,000 feet (10,200 meters) high!

Heracleion

This city, also known as Thonis, was once a Greek colony and later an important sea port in Egypt. In the eighth century, it sank into the Mediterranean and was entirely forgotten until it was rediscovered in 2000/2001.

Atolls are ring-shaped coral reefs that form after volcanic islands have sunk under the sea. They gradually grow up out of the ocean but only just peek out above the water's surface.

Volcanoes

The volcano Hunga Tonga-Hunga Ha'apai in the South Pacific is an underwater giant. Its peak is approximately 500 feet (150 meters) below sea level. An eruption in 2014 caused land to rise up from the sea, connecting the two neighboring islands Hunga Tonga and Hunga Ha'apai. A further eruption in 2022 caused the two islands to separate again.

663 feet
(202m)

Blue holes

Deep holes in the ocean floor are called blue holes. The deepest, at 663 feet (202 meters), is located in the Atlantic, close to the Bahamas. On the surface you can see a dark circle within the otherwise turquoise-blue water. At a depth of about 65 feet (20 meters) there is a giant underwater cave with a diameter of around 330 feet (100 meters). Blue holes are a source of fascination for many divers.

The Deep Sea

The deep sea is the largest part of our planet that has hardly been researched yet. It is blanketed in darkness and the water pressure is so high that divers would simply be squashed if they were to enter it—only deep-sea submarines are able to withstand the pressure.

Sperm whales hold a number of records: they are the largest toothed **whales**, have the largest brain of all living creatures, and can dive deeper and for longer than any other **mammal** (up to two hours!).

The spookfish has four eyes: two facing upward and two smaller eyes that face forward. This gives it a full view of its surroundings, allowing it to detect if a predator is drawing near.

The teeth of the Sloane's viperfish are so long that they poke out of its mouth, even when it is closed. It is able to produce light from photophores (light-producing organs) located along its sides.

The female anglerfish has a kind of fishing rod with an illuminated tip that extends from its forehead. It uses this to draw **prey** close to its mouth.

Vampire squid do not hunt living prey. They feed on marine snow—small particles that float in the water.

A depth of 33 feet (10 meters) signals the end of the "wave zone." At this level, submarines begin to float, the ocean appears turquoise, and the water is filled with animals and plants.

At 330 feet (100 meters), things start to get a little murkier and the water is a deep blue. Here you'll find jellyfish, **fish**, and sea grapes (salps). A salp's heart can change the direction of its blood flow.

The "deep sea" begins at 2,600 feet (800 meters) below the water's surface. The deeper you go, the colder and darker it gets. At some points it is totally dark, so the fish, jellyfish, and squid that live here generate their own light, either through a chemical process or using **bacteria.**

At about 16,000 feet (5,000 meters) below the surface lie the floors of the Pacific and the South Atlantic, which are home to sea cucumbers, anemones, and worms.

The ocean's deepest parts are over 35,000 feet (10,000 meters) down, such as the Mariana Trench or the Puerto Rico Trench. Shrimp-like creatures and sea cucumbers live here.

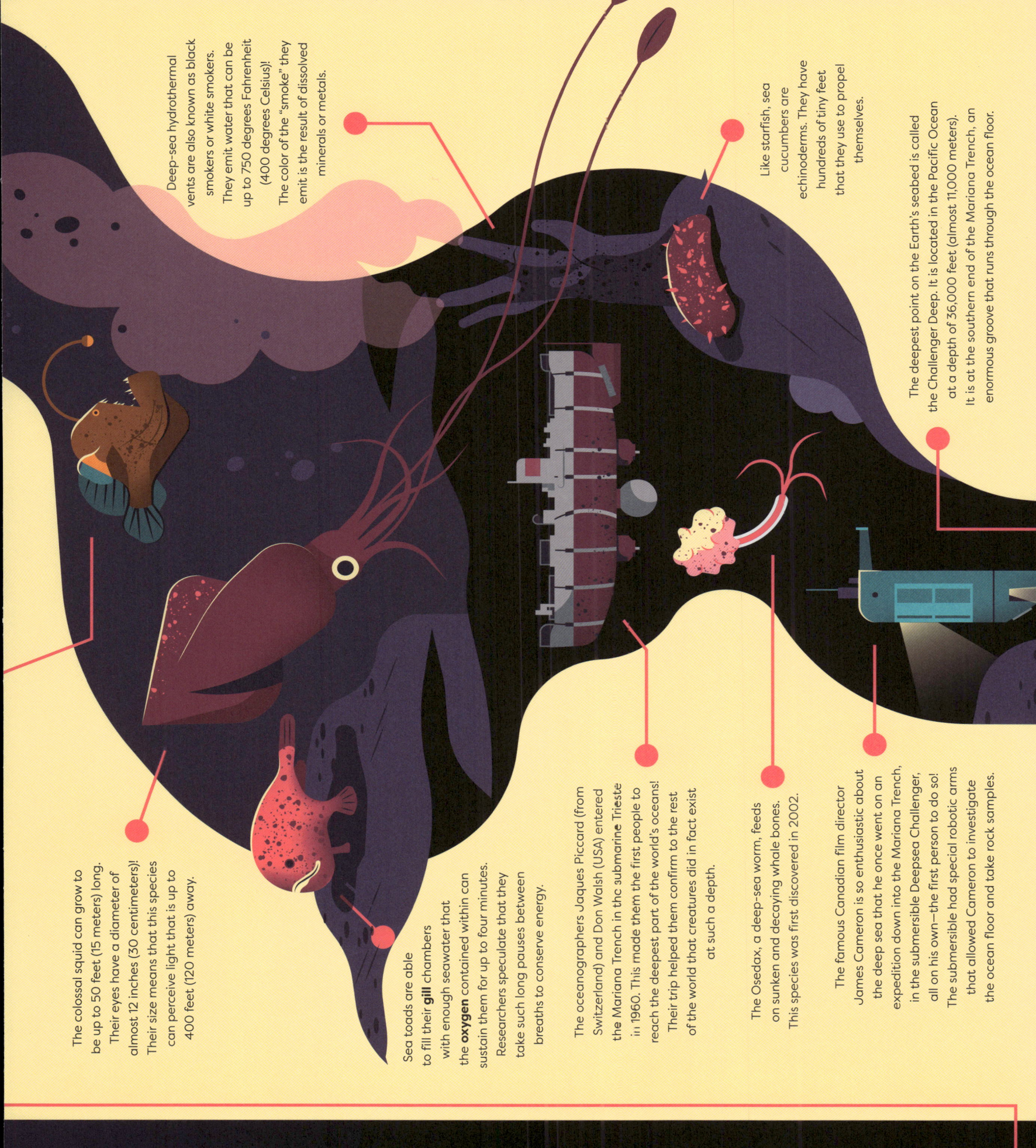

Deep-sea hydrothermal vents are also known as black smokers or white smokers. They emit water that can be up to 750 degrees Fahrenheit (400 degrees Celsius)! The color of the "smoke" they emit is the result of dissolved minerals or metals.

Like starfish, sea cucumbers are echinoderms. They have hundreds of tiny feet that they use to propel themselves.

The deepest point on the Earth's seabed is called the Challenger Deep. It is located in the Pacific Ocean at a depth of 36,000 feet (almost 11,000 meters). It is at the southern end of the Mariana Trench, an enormous groove that runs through the ocean floor.

The colossal squid can grow to be up to 50 feet (15 meters) long. Their eyes have a diameter of almost 12 inches (30 centimeters)! Their size means that this species can perceive light that is up to 400 feet (120 meters) away.

Sea toads are able to fill their **gill** chambers with enough seawater that the **oxygen** contained within can sustain them for up to four minutes. Researchers speculate that they take such long pauses between breaths to conserve energy.

The oceanographers Jaques Piccard (from Switzerland) and Don Walsh (USA) entered the Mariana Trench in the submarine Trieste in 1960. This made them the first people to reach the deepest part of the world's oceans! Their trip helped them confirm to the rest of the world that creatures did in fact exist at such a depth.

The Osedax, a deep-sea worm, feeds on sunken and decaying whale bones. This species was first discovered in 2002.

The famous Canadian film director James Cameron is so enthusiastic about the deep sea that he once went on an expedition down into the Mariana Trench, in the submersible Deepsea Challenger, all on his own—the first person to do so! The submersible had special robotic arms that allowed Cameron to investigate the ocean floor and take rock samples.

Humans and the Ocean

Humans live on the coast all around the world. For some, fishing or seafaring is a way of life, meaning that their livelihoods are closely connected to the health of the oceans. Some even live on the ocean itself. Follow Emma and Louis as they get to know some of these peoples.

Bajau

The Bajau people build their wooden houses on stilts in the shallow waters off the coast in the Pacific region. Imagine waking up in the morning and seeing a ray swimming in front of your house! Many Bajau learn to free-dive (which means they can swim underwater without diving equipment) as children—as adults, they are able to dive to depths of up to 230 feet (70 meters)!

Living along the west coast of North America from Alaska to British Columbia, the Tlingit, Haida, and Kwakiutl First Nation peoples traditionally fish using canoes.

Seafarers

Thousands of merchant vessels are active in the ocean every day. Their crews often spend months at a time on their ships before heading back to land.

Moken

The Moken people live on the ocean off the coast of Thailand and Myanmar, an area where there is a collection of many small and slightly larger islands known as the Mergui Archipelago. The Moken spend most of the year living on long wooden boats called kabangs. They are masters of spearfishing and diving.

Orang Laut

The Orang Laut are a nomadic people who live along the coast of Sumatra and Indonesia. Similar to the Moken and the Bajau, they possess incredible knowledge of the oceans and are extremely capable hunters and divers.

Inuit and Yupik

The Inuit live in Canada and Greenland, while the Yupik live in Alaska and Siberia. They are the original inhabitants of the Arctic and use kayaks and harpoons (barbed spears) to hunt seals, **whales,** and polar bears.

The elaborate art of tattooing practiced by Māori is much more than decoration. Each design reflects the history of the person who bears it and the position they hold within their community.

Māori

Māori are the tangata whenua (people of the land) of Aotearoa (New Zealand), and their culture is strongly connected with the ocean. Their ancestors reached the islands we now know as New Zealand at least 700 years ago on boats from the South Pacific.

Ocean Explorers

Vagn Walfrid Ekman (1874 – 1954)

Ekman conducted research into ocean currents and how they are influenced by the winds. In the process, he observed that icebergs don't drift in the direction of a prevailing wind but rather at an angle.

James Cook (1728 – 1779)

The British navigator undertook three major voyages in order to explore the Pacific, where he discovered many islands that were previously unknown to Europeans and had them added to maps. On December 24, 1777, he encountered a coral-based island that he named Christmas Island.

We use GPS-powered navigation devices, but back in the day seafarers used a compass to navigate. Magnetite, the mineral used in these, was first discovered in China in the twelfth century. How does it work? If a small piece is hung on some string it naturally orients itself according to the Earth's magnetic field, giving the user a north-south orientation.

The research submersible Shinkai 6500

Sylvia Earle (born 1935)

This US marine biologist has spent thousands of hours underwater researching the ocean. Together with her husband Graham Hawkes, she developed some of the technology required to explore the ocean's deepest points, where she found previously undiscovered springs, currents, and even creatures. She is responsible for the discovery of 154 species of plants and animals.

Jacques-Yves Cousteau (1910 – 1997)

The French oceanographer dedicated his life to investigating the underwater world. He made over 100 films on his expeditions. The submarine he built in 1959 (the SP-350 Denise) enabled two people to descend to a depth of up to 1,300 feet (350 meters) and observe the ocean's depths through windows only five inches (12 centimeters) in diameter. The submarine accompanied Cousteau's research ship Calypso and was used over 1,500 times. From 1962 Cousteau also worked with research stations located on the ocean floor.

Rachel Carson (1907 – 1964)

The US researcher published her first article about the natural world when she was only 10 years old. After completing her zoology studies, she began creating radio reports about the oceans and marine biology. Carson was also active in environmental-protection efforts and engaged in protests against pollution and the use of pesticides. Her work has directly influenced many people around the world to become involved in environmental movements.

Oceans at Risk

On their journey, Emma and Louis have discovered the most wonderful variety of plant and animal species, and learned a lot about the impact that the oceans' health has on our planet's **climate.** It is more important than ever to make sure these aquatic regions are protected.

Toxic substances

Unfortunately, oceans continue to be used like garbage dumps, with toxic waste from industrial production, oil, and sewage flowing into their waters. This causes animals and plants to suffer. Some species are even in danger of extinction as a result.

It is us humans who are responsible for the pollution and destruction of ocean environments. In order to improve ocean health, we have to change how we act.

Plastic

Plastic pollution poses a great threat to all oceans. All around the world there are giant plastic garbage patches that float across the water. Millions of marine animals have died as a result of their stomachs becoming clogged with plastic.

The so-called Great Pacific Garbage Patch, which stretches between California and Hawai'i, is 20 times as large as the US state of Maine! Plastic particles have been found in the deepest parts of the sea and even the Antarctic, as ocean currents distribute them all around the world.

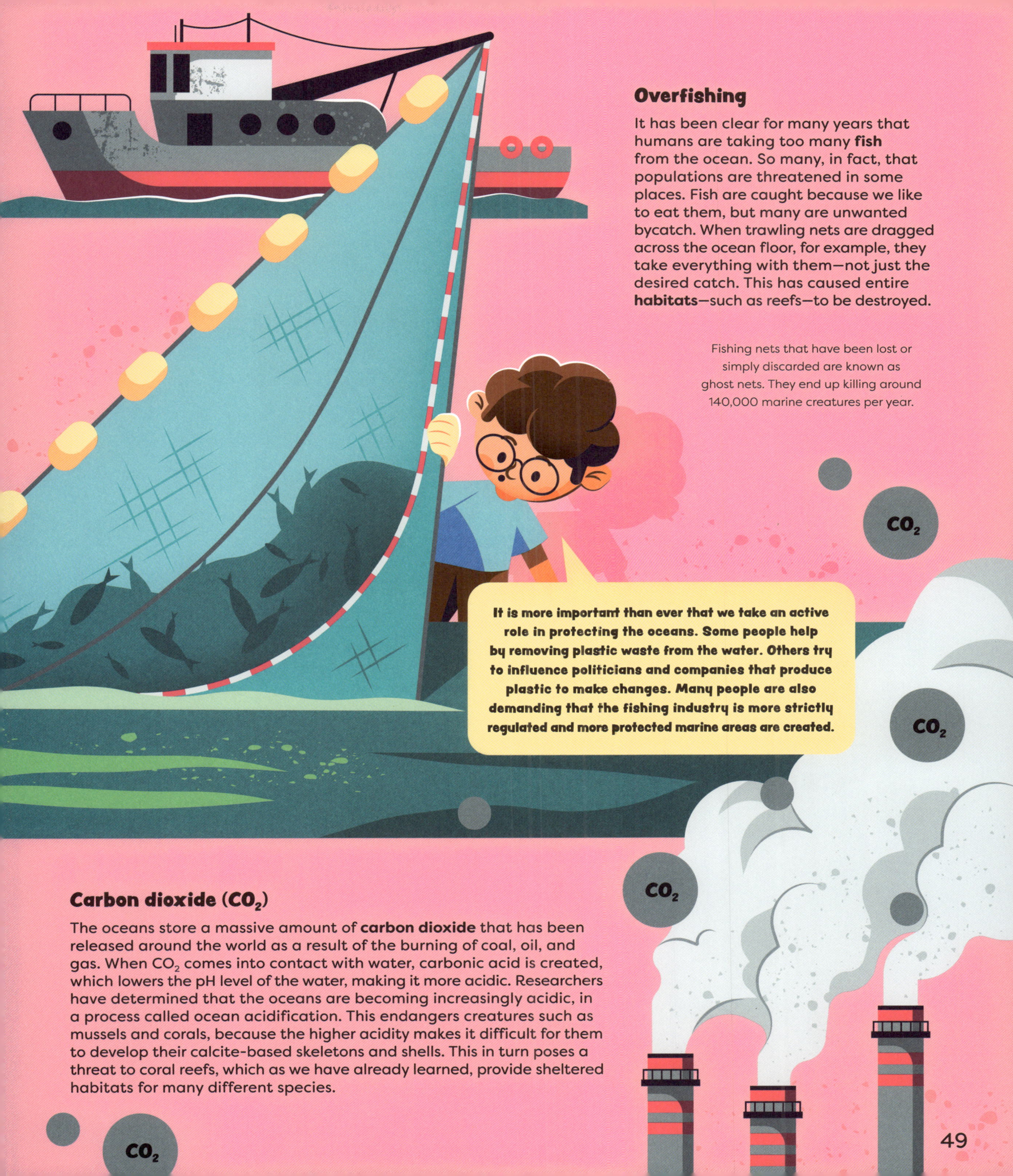

Overfishing

It has been clear for many years that humans are taking too many **fish** from the ocean. So many, in fact, that populations are threatened in some places. Fish are caught because we like to eat them, but many are unwanted bycatch. When trawling nets are dragged across the ocean floor, for example, they take everything with them—not just the desired catch. This has caused entire **habitats**—such as reefs—to be destroyed.

Fishing nets that have been lost or simply discarded are known as ghost nets. They end up killing around 140,000 marine creatures per year.

It is more important than ever that we take an active role in protecting the oceans. Some people help by removing plastic waste from the water. Others try to influence politicians and companies that produce plastic to make changes. Many people are also demanding that the fishing industry is more strictly regulated and more protected marine areas are created.

Carbon dioxide (CO₂)

The oceans store a massive amount of **carbon dioxide** that has been released around the world as a result of the burning of coal, oil, and gas. When CO$_2$ comes into contact with water, carbonic acid is created, which lowers the pH level of the water, making it more acidic. Researchers have determined that the oceans are becoming increasingly acidic, in a process called ocean acidification. This endangers creatures such as mussels and corals, because the higher acidity makes it difficult for them to develop their calcite-based skeletons and shells. This in turn poses a threat to coral reefs, which as we have already learned, provide sheltered habitats for many different species.

Nautical Tales

Stories about mysterious creatures that live in the ocean exist all around the world. Let's accompany Emma and Louis as they discover a few of them, as well as a couple of intrepid pirates.

Zheng Yi Sao

The pirate Zheng Yi Sao ruled the waves of the South China Sea in the nineteenth century. She had over 2,000 ships at her command and was notorious for the harsh punishments she dealt out when someone broke her rules. One rule dictated that her pirates were not allowed to harm women during attacks or if they were captured. She even stole treasure and ships from the emperor of China himself!

In the eighteenth century, a pirate by the name of Anne Bonny lived in the Caribbean. She was married to the pirate captain Calico Jack Rackham. Bonny plundered ships together with the pirate Mary Read and was a fearless fighter.

Edward Teach

The pirate Edward Teach—known as Blackbeard—was a greatly feared pirate of the eighteenth century because he attacked so many merchant ships, taking many prisoners in the process. The wreck of his ship Queen Anne's Revenge was discovered in the mid-1990s off the coast of North Carolina. A large number of weapons were found in the ruins—as well as gold.

According to a Chinese legend, jiaoren are merfolk that can weave "dragon silk," a unique and beautiful fabric that never gets wet. The jiaoren sold their wares by taking human form and going onto land.

Poseidon and Triton

In ancient times, the Greeks believed that the god Poseidon ruled the oceans. His son Triton, who lived in the depths of the ocean in a palace made of gold and coral, had a special twisted seashell that he could use to create giant waves or make the ocean perfectly still.

Sea monsters

Seafarers used to tell the story of the kraken (a giant, octopus-like creature), which lurked on the ocean floor and could devour entire ships. In Nordic countries there is a tale of an enormous sea serpent with a huge head and giant horns.

Mami Wata is a mermaid whose legend is told in Southern Africa. She has a serpent as a companion.

The ningyo of Japan are mermen with monkey-like mouths and very sharp teeth. Legend says they have magic powers and can unleash tsunamis when humans try to catch them—so don't even try it!

Ghost ships

For many centuries, seafarers told stories of ghost ships that would suddenly appear in the fog before disappearing. They were believed to bring bad luck. One particularly famous ghost ship was known as the Flying Dutchman: it could sail backwards, through storms, and even when there was no wind at all. Its captain was cursed and had to sail alone for all eternity, without being able to go ashore.

Farewell, Oceans!

Emma and Louis have traveled around the entire globe—from the Arctic to the Pacific—to investigate the oceans. They have encountered flying fish and deep-sea creatures that can generate their own light. And that's only a small taste of what they've found! The duo have also discovered that there is a great deal that we humans don't know about the oceans, because many parts have not been properly explored yet. But one thing quickly became clear to them during their adventures: it is very important that we protect the oceans, avoid polluting them, and don't catch too many fish. Each of us can—here and now—help deal with these issues in our daily lives. We need to do this, because the health of the oceans influences the lives of us all.

Glossary

Algae
Single or multicellular organisms that use sunlight to produce carbohydrates (glucose) from water and carbon dioxide. This process is called photosynthesis.

Bacteria
Tiny life-forms that consist of a single cell—although some do not even have a nucleus.

Birds
Vertebrate animals with feathers, wings, beaks, and two legs. Unlike mammals, who give birth to live young, birds lay eggs.

Carbon dioxide (CO$_2$)
A gas found in the air whose concentration in the atmosphere has greatly increased as a result of the burning of fossil fuels (such as coal or oil). This has caused the Earth's overall climate to change.

Centrifugal force
A force that occurs only during rotational and circular motions. It can be experienced on a chain carousel when it feels like you are flying out of the circle while turning.

Christopher Columbus
A famous Italian navigator who sailed by ship from Europe to the Americas.

Climate
The typical weather that usually occurs in a given place. Climates can be warm, cold, dry, or moist. This largely depends on a place's distance from the equator (near to the equator it is both hot and moist).

Colony
A group of creatures that live together.

Earth's rotation
As well as orbiting around the Sun over the course of a year, the Earth also rotates about its own axis, completing one full rotation in a day.

Echolocation
This refers to the process of locating objects by emitting sound waves and then listening to the reflected sounds. Numerous animals use this technique to orient themselves or to locate their next meal.

Endemic
When life-forms only exist in one specific place on Earth.

Equator
An imaginary line that encircles the Earth and divides it into two sections: the northern and southern hemispheres.

Evaporation
The process by which a substance changes state from a liquid to a gas.

Fish
Vertebrate animals with scales that live in water, breathe through gills, and move about using their fins.

GPS
GPS is short for global positioning system. By receiving signals from multiple satellites, a GPS device is able to precisely pinpoint a person's or an object's location. Ships and cars, for example, are often equipped with GPS receivers. It is possible to locate people and animals (whether pets or wild animals) if they are carrying/fitted with a GPS device.

Gills
Organs that aquatic animals use to "breathe in" oxygen from the water.

Gravitational force
Often referred to as gravity, this is the phenomenon of attraction between objects that have mass. On Earth, gravitational force is experienced as weight—the more mass an object has, the greater the gravitational force, and hence weight, it will have.

Habitat
The environment in which a creature lives—or in some cases, in which a range of different creatures live together.

Incubation
The protection and warming of eggs so that they can develop properly. At the end of the incubation phase, one or more young hatchlings emerge from their eggs.

Invertebrates
Animals that do not have a spine, such as insects, spiders, and worms.

Mammals
Warm-blooded vertebrate animals that have hair and feed their young using the milk that they produce.

Nutrients
Substances such as minerals, vitamins, carbohydrates, fats, and proteins that are necessary for the growth and survival of life-forms.

Oxygen
A gas found in the air that is necessary for most forms of life to exist.

Photosynthesis
A process by which animals and algae generate carbohydrates from a combination of water, carbon dioxide, and sunlight. The green pigment we see in plants and algae is called chlorophyll. Chlorophyll absorbs light, and the energy gained from this is used to convert carbon dioxide (as well as water) into glucose. Oxygen is also created as a byproduct of this process and then released back into the atmosphere.

Plankton
Tiny organisms in the water that serve as food for many marine animals.

Polyp
A creature that lives attached to the ocean floor and belongs to the family of cnidaria. Some polyps join forces to create colonies.

Prey
These are animals that serve as food for predators.

Reptiles
Vertebrate animals like lizards, snakes, turtles, and crocodiles. They mostly live on land and have scales instead of feathers or hair.

Tentacles
Long and nimble limbs that animals or plants use to catch prey.

Tides
The ebb and flow of the oceans. When it is high tide the seas rise; at low tide they shrink away from the coast. Both are caused by the Moon, whose gravitational force draws the water toward it.

Vertebrates
Animals that have a spine, such as fish, amphibians, reptiles, birds, and mammals.

Whales
Large mammals that live in the ocean. Dolphins also belong to the same family as whales (Cetacea).

Zooids
A tiny animal that is part of a larger colony of these animals, which form bodies, like jellyfish, corals, polyps, and sea anemones.

Explore the Ocean
Adventures Under the Sea
with Emma and Louis

Written by Anne Ameri-Siemens
Illustrated by Anton Hallmann

This book was conceived, edited,
and designed by Little Gestalten.

Edited by Robert Klanten, Fay Evans,
and Richard Schmädicke

Translation from German by Ryan Eyers

Layout by Melanie Ullrich

Typefaces: Calcine by Mark Frömberg
Filson Soft by Olivier Gourvat
Peachy Keen JF by Jason Walcott

Printed by Schleunungdruck GmbH, Marktheidenfeld
Made in Germany

Published by Little Gestalten, Berlin, 2023
ISBN 978-3-96704-750-9

For more information, and to order books, please visit:
little.gestalten.com

Bibliographic information published by the Deutsche Nationalbibliothek.
The Deutsche Nationalbibliothek lists this publication in the
Deutsche Nationalbibliografie; detailed bibliographic data are available online at dnb.de.

This book was printed on paper certified according to the standards of the FSC®.

Explore other titles from the series!

Explore
the World
Discoveries that
shaped our world

ISBN: 978-3-96704-703-5

Explore
the Rainforest
Emma and Louis
in the Jungle

ISBN: 978-3-96704-719-6

Anne Ameri-Siemens is an award-winning writer who tells whimsical stories about the world around us. Anne lives in Berlin but would like to spend more time by the ocean. This is her third book with Little Gestalten.

Anton Hallmann was born in Brandenburg, Germany, and studied illustration at the Hamburg University of Applied Sciences. He lives in Stockholm, Sweden, with his wife and their bunnies. After *Explore the World* and *Explore the Jungle,* this is his third children's book.